The Lie The Devil Told Me & I Believed

BUT GOD

By Stephanie D. Stamps

Acknowledgments

To My Children: **Andrea, Adrienne, Salena & Stephen**, thank you for your collaboration with God and for choosing me as your vessel for birth. And thank you for bringing out the most Love I could ever have.

To My god Sister, **Trudy L Hopkins,** who always pulled me back in and told me the truth whether I wanted to hear it or not.

To **My Parents**, Thank You

To **Sparkle Smith** My Destiny helper.

To those who have poured into my life knowingly and unknowingly:

Apostle Leroy Thompson

Bishop TD Jakes

Jaunita Bynum

Marianne Williamson

Dr. Cindy Trimm

Joyce Myers

Dr. Gaylena White

Dr. Tiffany K. Jordan

And to all my **family, friends,** and the list goes on and on, and there is not enough room to add all of you, but you all know who you are: Thank You!

'O you afflicted one, Tossed with Tempest, and not comforted, Behold, I will lay your stones with colorful gems, and lay your foundations with sapphires. I will make your pinnacles of rubies, Your gates of crystal, And all your walls of precious stones. Isaiah 54:11-12

Table of contents

Introduction

Sometimes you have to go back to go forward.

In my case, I went back to my experiences, my choices, and my childhood so I could be free.

I was told once to be careful who you tell your Dear John story to. But I believe without honesty, there is no stability or true freedom.

Freedom was always important to me, and I didn't know why. But there was always something inside of me whispering the truth that I needed to be free. I could hear even the faintest whisper of freedom. Even if the whisper seemed far away I could still hear it!

I know now. Truth be told, I always did. Subconsciously and spiritually because I was and we are designed to be free, keyword to BE: *(an action verb) to occur, take place, to exist, to occupy oneself.*

We all have assignments in life, and others depend on our freedom. We have a responsibility to be the best of who we are called to be.

We are not our own. God uses us for our good and His Glory. Jesus got on the Cross for that very reason and instructed us not to get in bondage again, Galatians 5:1. Our Heavenly Father sent His only begotten Son for this very purpose.

For God so Loved The World That he gave his only begotten son that whoever believes in him should not perish but have everlasting life.

John 3:16 NKJV

But things happen along the way, life as some of us call it. We do some things to ourselves (choices), and others are chosen for us. It happens to us.

This book is not about what someone has done to me. This book is about the lie the devil or our enemy told me, the lie that I believed.

You see, we have choices to believe what God said about us, the truth or the lie the devil said about us: distorted truth. If you believe the lie is true, then it's true. Your life and decisions will reflect the lie you believe. If you believe the truth, then you believe what God said, and your life will reflect that.

For as he thinks in his heart so is He.

Proverbs 23:7 NKJV

Imagine when I had to come to grips with the fact that I believed the lie. You may ask how I did I know? I looked at my life and my choices. The evidence of my life and choices spoke for themselves. Now by most standards, I don't have a bad life. But when you know you are not operating to your full potential, it creates a conviction to level up.

I knew there were some blocks/strongholds in my life. Being frustrated because you are not in your full potential can be challenging. This challenging dilemma can cause much heartache and pain (and it can deeply hurt your feelings).

I was so frustrated with always starting over. So I began to search. I searched for answers through prayer, books, sermons, energy cleansing, yoga, deliverance, meditation; you name it!

You see, I knew God but did I believe God? That belief system is a mighty thing that must be renewed.

And do not be conformed to this world, but be transformed by the renewing of your mind, that you may prove what is that good and acceptable and perfect will of God.

Romans 12:2 NKJV

It's not that you are such a bad person, and the man in a red suit with horns is holding you. No! There are deceptive/blinding situations we get ourselves into. Oftentimes we get in the thick of it. In that thick place, we can't see ourselves in the deception/blind spots because, many times, we do not realize we are in this place. You never see yourself in it (that blind/deceptive place). And when you can't see yourself in it, then God can't get it (the deliverance) to you. It's like you're playing life and not living up to your full potential of life when you know there's more.

Once you speak out into to the universe, that which God has created for you (to have dominion in), then you will recognize and receive from Him. You will receive from God the revelation of all He has for you and wants to give to you freely. But if you can't conceptualize the revelation and accept it as yours (deliverance, destiny, and blessings), it has nowhere to come!

The enemy wants to distort your view. Take for example, Jesus and the blind man of Bethseda.

He took the blind man by the hand and led him outside the village. When He had spit on the man's eyes and put his hands on him, Jesus asked, do you see anything? He looked up and said, "I see people: they look like trees walking around."

Mark 8:23-24 NIV

The enemy tried to cause me to hide, to change who I am (the true person); the true spirit of who I Am. I use these examples of my life as my testimony, not to show you the person, but the entry, the door/ experiences used to get into my life.

These are doors used to manipulate choices and decisions to ultimately change your walk/ direction. These doors are accessed to abort the calling of your destiny.

This is the opposite of what God wants for us: God wants us to trust Him. He wants to trust us with what He has called us to and predestined us to do. All of Heaven is rooting for us to fulfill our purpose. The whole world is waiting for us.

For the earnest expectation of the creation eagerly waits for the revealing of the sons of God.

Romans 8:19 NKJV

What I have found to be true is that no matter what happens we are ultimately responsible for ourselves. We are responsible for our spirituality, growth, and our truth (and search thereof). No everlasting blame game allowed.

The situations, the circumstances, and the traumas may explain (the method). But to be truly free, we can't use it (the blame game). However, pinpointing the root causes opens the pathway to our freedom.

I heard this in an interview. And it rang true to my Spirit. You have to tell your story or your truth until it doesn't make you cringe anymore. You have to tell your truth until it liberates you. Blaming runs out; you have to do the work of deliverance, healing or therapy. Sometimes all three are necessary for your complete recovery. They all (deliverance, healing and therapy) go hand in hand. This is because blocks and barriers have to go. It's a must for wholeness.

I had to take a look at or face the traumas and the situations and circumstances. I had to take a look at how this trauma made me feel and what it did to me. I had to examine what the damage was. I had to evaluate the damage's impact on my life.

You would do (evaluate) this for a car or a house. Why would you not do it for yourself? This allowed me to step out of it and look at it through the lenses of God's eyes and not a victim's eyes.

It's like calling an insurance adjuster (Jesus is the adjuster in this case). We are called to go beyond the mediocre. Our belief systems have to change and align with the word of God. Our soul and our body has to get into alignment with our spirit. These three should follow the Holy Spirit. Be led by the Spirit, the Holy Spirit. The Holy Spirit is the spirit of truth, the guide, the comforter.

I will not leave you orphan; I will come to you.

John 14:18 NKJV

With every experience of brokenness the enemy meant for my destruction, BUT GOD meant for my good and his glory. If we could just remember, we win. I won! Every fragment of my life will not be wasted, and yours shall not be wasted either!

Chapter 1

In The Beginning

Cornbread

1 Cup of cornmeal

1 Cup of flour

¾ Cup of sugar

2 Eggs

1 Cup milk

Tbsp. baking powder

Tsp salt

Food has a way of bringing people together. It is a wonderful thing when we break bread. This is even scriptural, according to Acts 2:46-47. Also, in 2nd Corinthians 9:10, it indicates that those who supply bread for food enlarge the harvest of your righteousness. Does that mean that because I cook and supply cornbread that I will enlarge your righteousness? No!

But there is spiritual food and natural food. As a chef, I supply natural food, which is great for fellowship. However, it is the Lord who supplies the spiritual bread/food.

There is physical bread and spiritual bread. We know this because, in the book of Matthew, Jesus is referred to as the bread of life.

Everyone loves my cornbread. I have been cooking it since eight years old. It was my grandmother's cornbread recipe and has been a demand for me to cook it as well as cornbread dressing.

There are many benefits of eating cornbread. Cornbread is vegetable-rich and can be very nutritious. Cornbread is very economical and can be made in various forms (fluffy loaves, fried or high rising). Cornbread was very popular during the

Civil War for the fact that it was economical. Not only was it economical but delicious.

Cornbread was used as nourishment for soldiers who were fighting a war. Normally, a war is fought for freedom and justice. Freedom and justice comes to break shackles, strongholds, bondages and mindsets decades and centuries old. What shackles, bondages, century and decade-old mindsets do you need to let go of? What nourishment can be provided to give you the strength to break the chains and enter into freedom? The word of God is spiritual food; and Christ is the bread of life.

The definition of BUT: used to introduce a phrase or clause contrasting with what has already been mentioned: Except, apart from, other than. But is a conjunction used to introduce something contrasting with what has already been mentioned.

But means "except." The reason why something didn't happen: BUT GOD. God always intervenes and delivers and liberates you no matter how impactful your experience. He is the force behind the force.

No weapon formed against you shall prosper.

First sentence of

Isaiah 54:17NKJV

He is saying I am a bigger force. No matter what rises against you, he will vindicate you.

BUT GOD

Chapter 2

Witness

Snicker Doodles Cookie Recipes

Flour

Sugar

Butter

Cinnamon

Eggs

Cream OF Tarter

Cinnamon Sugar

Baking Soda

Vanilla

One of the healthiest ingredients in snickerdoodle cookies is cinnamon. Cinnamon has many benefits. Cinnamon is antiviral and antibacterial, which means it can fight off viruses and infections. Cinnamon can improve gut health and reduce high blood pressure.

Cinnamon relieves digestive discomfort and lowers blood sugar. Cinnamon can also lower the risk of type- two diabetes. Cinnamon has many healing properties. Just like cinnamon can heal the body and the gut, the Holy Spirit and the word can heal the spiritual gut or your spirit man.

Cinnamon can heal the body, and Christ can heal the body and the soul. Cinnamon fights off infections, and God is the man of war who will fight your battles!

The Spirit Himself bears witness with our spirit that we are children of God, Romans 8:16 NKJV

Doors: There were some early childhood traumas and traumas that happened to me in school. So there were struggles in my perspective of learning as a child, which I was embarrassed about.

So because I was embarrassed, I would not ask for help. I felt I could not ask for help at home or at school. I hid it and learned a memorization system of how to get through each day. Needless to say, school was exhausting, and I was not fond of school at all.

I knew school was a necessity. I wanted to like school; I mean because it was the thing to do, LOL. I mean, it's what my parents would want. By the way, my parents are super smart. But there were definitely some blocks for me.

A great example of what I was going through, can today, be compared to dyslexia. In those days, either you knew it, or you were placed in the slow class. That's what they called it then. Or they just thought that you were just lazy. I was neither, and I knew it. But my self-esteem took a hit. Can you see the amount of work it took for me to go to school each day?

One of the reasons it took me so long to write this book is I told God, you want me to do what? You know I can't spell. I'm a horrible speller. You are the omnipresent God, you know my situation. Just like Moses when God told Moses to go and talk to the pharaoh. He told God I have a speech impediment. So what Moses actually said to God was, "I'm slow of tongue" Exodus 4:10.

My Moses experience was with Ms. Barns, my 6th-grade teacher! We all have that one teacher that makes that difference in your life. When God sends someone into your life for assistance, one of your destiny helpers, it's a relief. However, that does not mean it will always be easy. You are still the one who has to do the work.

But it somewhat makes the process smoother or easy in the sense that your ram in the bush can also be your destiny helper. Your destiny helper has the ability to bring the best out in you. Ms. Barns would not allow me to give her the minimum. This is because her expectations of me were high. Your destiny helper can bring out the best in you because they see the best in you. They envision your success before it manifests. They are the people that come to help midwives or birth out the best part of you to help you go to your next level.

Oh, but there were still some battles! But my destiny helper (Ms. Barnes) prevailed. She was not having it. She could discern the opportunities that could bring out the best out in me. She put me in charge of a field trip to the park.

I had to plan the route we were going to take. I had to plan what to bring, the time we left, and the time we returned. I had to pass out the field trips slips and retrieve them with parental signatures. I had to ensure we were all on time for the events of the day.

I also had to plan the "what if" (the plan B's): what if someone forgets their field trip slip, if someone forgets their baseball mitts, etc. I was responsible for improvising the "what ifs." How she knew I could do that, I do not know. I guess she just knew I could do it. I felt I could do it too!

I just didn't have an opportunity to demonstrate it until Ms. Barns. But I took the opportunity Ms. Barns provided. And she did not micromanage me. She knew I did not need to be micromanaged. I despise being micro-managed to this day!

The trip was a success. It was my point of contact with success. Like the lady with the issue of blood, she said if I could just touch the hymn of His garment. It was a point of contact. It was a transfer of power between Ms. Barns and I. Ms. Barns empowered me to be the best I could be. She knew I was creative, and she looked at my learning from a point of what I loved. How do I continue this point of contact with success after the school year with Ms. Barns and Middle School begins?

Middle school is a critical time of identity and discovery. However, I could not find my point of contact. This began my rebellious days. Rebellion is a process for most children. But there is a root behind it. When rebellion goes beyond teenage years: the root is fear.

I learned another lie/deception during these years. The lie/deception was: "I could handle it. You know, like the Michael Jackson song, I'm bad." That's me. I got it. Things happened that should not have happened. But I can handle it! So I thought.

But what this did was shape my viewpoint. My perception was off. I became involved in an abusive relationship that actually started in High School. I was so stressed. I was pregnant at 17 and out of my parents' house by 18! But I'm bad, and I can handle it. Lies from the pit of Hell! This continued throughout my early twenties and it ended there.

The person who is supposed to cover/protect you cannot be the violator. As I look for my lesson, I married a person at 18 to leave my parents' home to someone who was abusing me. I had some responsibility for myself that I did not accept.

Knowing my faults or brokenness does not give anyone the permission to abuse me or anyone else. I must look at myself. Why was I there? I remember the first time someone told me, "you are in an abusive relationship, this is domestic violence." I was indignant! What are you talking about? I fight back! Ha! Ha! How can you be in a fight and lose all the time? How can you be in a fight just because the sky is blue? We would get into fights about any little thing.

God or the enemy sends someone. The question should be "Who sent you?"

But I must look at myself. Why was I there? I was looking for someone broken to mend my brokenness. Why choose this person or why choose this? It was a familiar spirit.

Subconsciously, we always know the truth. It is the lack of courage or bondage that keeps you from standing in your truth. The soul tie has been broken.

I did not recognize I was afraid because I always equated fear as physical. I was looking on the outside when I should have been looking on the inside. But if you are only getting glimpses of who you truly are, then you are and living under a false identity. The perception of who you are is distorted, and off course.

I didn’t realize it until I started having severe panic attacks. One thing about panic attacks is that they are usually not about the current state that you’re in. It's about the hidden post-trauma and stress from childhood to adulthood. It's about un-dealt with issues of which you may be unaware of and some you may be aware of. The un-dealt with issues then become triggers. Your current state may trigger the attack. However, your current state is only the surface of the deep-seated stronghold of trauma.

Particularly for Black women, the fear they have had to face, endure and keep silent about is due to our history of oppression. Because of this, Black women or women, in general, can develop a mindset/coping mechanism that says: “I can handle it or I got this.” And you just go on, or you think to yourself: I don't have time to be falling apart. In our culture, yes, this is true. We had to be strong. We as a people have endured some things that are unspeakable, and yes, we are strong!

I am strong! But it is still unprocessed trauma, generational and demonic strongholds that do not allow you to live life to your full potential.

Life can be based on familiarity. We are human beings who act like human doings. I wrote a journal about the B's (pronounced bees) being, believing, becoming, belonging, and obedience. Yahweh God is who he is, and the definition of Yahweh is to be. We have existed as God has created us before the foundation of the world.

Before I formed you in the womb I knew you; before you were born I sanctified you; I ordained you a prophet to the nations (purpose-driven).

Jeremiah 1:5. NKJV

BUT GOD

Chapter 3

Holy

Grandma's Chicken & Dumplings

Chicken

Salt

Pepper

Water

Onions

Bay leaves

Celery

Chicken and dumplings are a healthy source of protein and nutrients needed for energy and good health. Chicken and dumplings also contain iron, a mineral that assists in oxygen support and red blood cell

transformation. In other words, it can help renew your heart by transforming blood cells.

My grandmother's rule about chicken & dumplings was not to overwork that dough and make it tough and thick. I would watch her make those dumplings like I would watch her make cornbread. She said it should not be too thick and should have the right bite and texture.

I remember chewing the dumpling and knowing it was the right bite and texture. She gave examples of how it should taste. For example, *if it was too wet, it would be like this or if it was too dry, it would be like that.*

Her dough was flour and water, with the exception of a pinch of salt. But it was the consistency and technique. Not too much salt because the seasoning came from her chicken stock. She would always put onion and celery in her water to boil her chicken, other than salt and pepper. But I tweaked it a little bit and added garlic and bay leaves. In my dough, I added parsley, so my dumpling had green flakes.

It was like taking your chicken and dumplings to another level. Once the chicken had cooked, it was taken out the chicken stock while the stock was still boiling. My grandmother stated it should have a rapid boil. Once the flour and the dough were cooking, it had to have a thickening, as my grandmother called it.

I needed to keep a nice stir as it was boiling. I then turn it down to a simmer and put a lid on it so the dumplings could cook. After the dumplings cook, you can return the chicken to the pot.

I would always serve dumplings with cornbread, and pickled beets. My mother's mother kept a jar of pickled beets in her refrigerator. It was truly farm-to-table. The combination of cornbread, pickled beets and dumplings was the ultimate comfort food. Not because of the actual meal but because of the lineage of the meal. The meal is a combination of both my mother and father's mothers (so both sides of my generation).

As you pray for generational strongholds to be broken, you may not even know what they are or how they came in. However, you do know that something is blocked. Recognize that you are the link and the thread between your children and your parents.

You may not even recognize this place you hold (link/thread). However, it does not have to be that way when you receive an awareness of the light. You are called to break the generational strongholds so the present and your future can be broken from the past. You are the missing link, the stronghold breaker. You are not only the stronghold breaker, you also weave the generational blessings back together in harmony.

These (chicken dumplings and pickled beets) were two of both my grandmother's favorites, and I combined them (pickled beets, cornbread and dumplings). Just as I served this meal to my children, they didn't know where these three favorites came from. All they knew is this was what I was serving. It is my job to serve the next generation their freedom.

I heard a story once that a minister shared; the story of a woman. The woman always cooked ham in a small pot. Someone asked her why she always cooks the ham in the small pot? She said, "that is the way my mother always did it." She researched that the only reason her mother did it that way was because her mom could not afford a larger pot.

However, this woman could afford a larger pot, but she still did it the way her mother did it. Metaphorically, some of us are too big for the small spaces we have forced ourselves into in order to accommodate a custom or tradition.

She was suppressing the meal when she no longer had to. Once she came into the awareness of why her mom cooked the ham that way, she did not have to continue doing it that way.

That is the same way with generational strongholds. Once you understand, you don't have to stay in a certain mindset. You can experience freedom. Once you get a revelation of that freedom, you accept the fact that certain things do not have to be the same way they have been generational. You no longer see these things as traditions or "just the way it is." Because they are hindrances, it's up to you to continue to fight to break the strongholds. Just like this meal was the perfect combination of three, the trinity (Father, Son and Holy Spirit) is the perfect combination for your life.

The Father, Son and Holy Spirit

The same fulfillment that took place in this meal should also happen between you, the Father, Son and Holy Spirit. When you have all three in your life, there should be a perfect balance. The triangle is the strongest angle. That's not by coincidence. There are three sides. Your interaction with the Father, Son and Holy Spirit is about relationships.

The combination of the meal was about relationships. Our relationships should be God-ordained. This does not mean ***halo status***. Have the best intentions for both parties involved. Be clear and intentional about your relationships.

An evil doer gives heed to false lips; A liar listens eagerly to a spiteful tongue.

Proverbs 17:4 NKJV

For God is not a God of disorder but of peace, as in all the meetings of God's holy people.

1st Corinthians 14:33.NIV

Therefore, relationships are critical to your life, purpose and destiny.

Doors:

Condemnation, Guilt, Shame & Self- Betrayal

All of my relationships were not bad. Some of them were good, but I had no trust. I not only distrusted the other person but also myself. I feared that I would make the same decision again and that I might choose wrong. I have been in a few rough ones. I think I drew some of those to me, just so I can show them who I was (Ludacris) right.

That is like jumping into a fire pit and saying, “I bet you can’t burn me because I’ll do this to you.” And the fire is saying to you, “you will do what? I’m the fire!” You don’t control this. I (the fire) do!

Sometimes we do things to ourselves because we have the wrong information about ourselves. So we make wrong decisions and choices, and they have consequences. We base it on a fact (situation). We are not a situation! I'm paraphrasing this, but whose report are you going to believe, the Lord's or the World's?

I never wanted to be aligned as a victim or to be seen as weak, so I hid these things. I had good intentions but the wrong perspective. By hiding, this made me a victim. I hid what I was going through in my marriage/relationships and what I went through as a single parent. So that made me a victim by default. But power can come after a default! The power comes from your testimony and your truth Victim root word 15th century: a creature killed as a religious sacrifice. The Latin word victim: A living creature killed and offered as a sacrifice to a deity of supernatural power or in the performance of a religious ritual. Current definition: a person hardened, injured or killed as a result of a crime, accident or other event or action or (tricked).

The enemy can do nothing but trick you because he can't create anything new, so it has to be trickery. (I found it amazing that the words trick and perspective are a part of being a victim.)This is why it is important to heal. Your soul and your spirit should not be in alignment with or identified as being a victim.

What was it that you were in toxic alignment with knowingly or unknowingly? Take search:

Search me oh Lord and know my heart, try me and know my anxieties: And see if there is any wicked way in me, and lead me in the way of everlasting. Psalm 139:23-24NKJV

It's not that a situation did not happen: it's the alignment with it. How do you associate or identify or align yourself with your situation: past, present or future?

If we could just look at our situation with a new perspective! You may have been taught, or deceived, or even made a free-will decision that taking care of others or putting others before self was the norm. I was very good at taking care of others and their needs. I was not so good at taking care of myself and my needs. This causes resentment. The intention may be good on your part. However, if self -care is not a part of your routine emptiness can happen,

There is an expectation of continuing with this false perception. This false perception makes you feel as though you are wonderful because you do this. It is actually manipulative, so when you are not doing it, you feel guilty or shamed. Then your identity becomes wrapped in it.

Three words here are not in alignment with God's word: manipulative, guilt and shame. So caring for someone or something should not cause you to disintegrate mentally, physically or spiritually.

Know this: this is not a license to be selfish, and this does not take away from being giving or the attitude of: "I got mine, you get yours."

As I have said before, we have assignments, and we are of service. We are not our own. But when you say no to someone else, they should respect your boundaries. You are not a sacrificial lamb. Jesus was the sacrifice.

Resentment and Distorted Self Perception

Anything that kills your spirit or puts you at risk, it is out of order. You will end up empty, and you cannot pour out from an empty vessel. Then this causes resentment: another door. Do you see the web? It was to the point where caring for myself almost looked as though it was foreign.

You are not to sacrifice yourself for others. It becomes a distorted view of yourself and your identity, and it is deception at its finest. I got this revelation when I kept coming up empty in relationships, and I had to assess why I was choosing the same type of person. Your self-perception dictates the type of relationships you pick, whether the relationships are business or personal. So if you have a distorted self -perception, you will overlook that a person could only give you 10% in a relationship although you require 90%.

It is a must that you begin to look at yourself and the thread in you that is drawn to the other person. This thread can become aligned with your belief system and can change with perception. If you no longer align and identify with it, it is no longer working.

You cannot sacrifice yourself to fit into someone else's box. You cannot continue to remain in the dark to make someone else feel good about who they are. You must be true to thine own self. It makes no sense to knowingly stay in darkness. You can't stay in the dark for anyone! *Be true to thine own self.*

BUT GOD

Chapter 4

Seasons

Spaghetti and Bolognese Sauce

Peppers: Green, Yellow, Red

Garlic

Marinara sauce

Parmesan Cheese

Sundried Tomatoes

Ground Beef

Italian Sausage

Stewed Tomatoes

Basil

Italian Seasoning

Olive Oil

Salt and Pepper to Taste

Spaghetti is the easiest meal to make for children. You know they are all going to eat it.

Train up a child in the way he should go. And when he is old he will not depart from it.

Proverbs 22:6 NKJV

The seeds are dropped literally. What seeds did I drop or deposit into My Children? Or what seed/seeds were they exposed to in life or even generationally? These seeds were no fault of their own.

No matter how wonderful we think our children are; (and they are pretty wonderful, they are a blessing) children do not wear halos. If you see your child with a halo, you cannot see the truth and make the proper corrections for their growth. Therefore, that type of mindset can hinder your parenting (just my opinion).

What seed have you deposited into your children knowingly or unknowingly? Know this. The person will return to what was planted because it is familiar. You know that thing you say to yourself. Why do I keep doing this to myself? It is familiar, and you may not recognize the tie or connection until you look at the root of it.

The influence of that root in your life can definitely change. As soon as it is no longer allowed to hide, it is exposed. It has no legal right.

The Lord gave instructions, “train” instructions: knowledge, wisdom and understanding. God wants us to walk in light, awareness and the fullness thereof. So He knew there needed to be some teaching involved.

Preferably teaching should be led by the Holy Spirit. But we all know we have free will. I heard the best line in a movie:

“You are not your children's only influence in life.” As much as we would want for our children or to raise/train our children, we are not their only influence.

And the best earthly advice I received was from my earthly parents. They said some impactful/influential things to their twenty -three-year-old daughter (who stood before them with 4 children). Their daughter was returning home from an abusive marriage with no job; no money and no place of her own. My father also told me not to marry that person. I’m just saying!

One piece of advice my mother shared with me was that “All children must have some successes.”

The most impactful advice my father gave me was, "Find a church and raise your children in it. If you don’t raise them, the world will raise them. Either way, it goes, somebody is going to raise them. Who do you want it to be? You are responsible for them. Others may help, but they are yours.

You are their parent. This is your responsibility. Your responsibilities are there Mental, Spiritual and Physical health: their overall wellbeing."

I know now that the atmosphere/environment (even if you never say a word), the energy of what your children physically see and hear, affects their belief system.

Most people do the best that they can as parents. I said! "most parents." But as a parent you have to recognize that you may be getting yourself together or moved on and matured from your past decisions. However, many times our children can be left as collateral damage. However, I had my checklist, and I was ready to go. This parenting thing! LOL

Can you believe this? There were a lot of discouraging words spoken to me and about me. Can you believe that!

You know the typical stereotypes: things said about my age, race, education and financial limits, etc. Some of the statements/seeds that were trying to be dropped (door): "I don't know how you are going to make it." And therefore, this sparked single mom seeds of abandonment: rejection, fear, and shame into my spirit and soul.

I despised it. This made me feel as though I was weak or a victim in someone else's eyes. It made me feel as though people thought my children were going to be less than (in their minds). I did not want to identify with that. I always felt this was not true. So now I am full of anger. Now I have identified myself with "I will show you!" This was more so pride, and not in a good way. At this point, I am really hiding now! I would have never asked or let anyone know I needed help. I needed food stamps, and I would go so far out of the way to the store so no one would know I had them. This was another self-accepting lie: (deception) and the Mission begins.

If you could picture the mission impossible music for a moment: LOL. I was never ashamed of my children. I was never ashamed to be out of an abusive marriage. Confusing right? This is because the world wanted me to be ashamed of being a single parent. But what was the alternative? Return to an abusive marriage. NO! Just to say what! Or just to make others more comfortable about my life? No!

I believe in marriage and family as one of the most important things in the world.

God, Family, Body of Christ/ church and Career. But what if any of these (except for God) are killing your mind body or soul? NO, and NO again, NO. For me, I found another point of contact for success. I am good at this mommy thing. I got this parenting thing down.

Ok, except these are human beings with their own soul and mind, their own path that I am trying to guide.

I really wasn't a free-will kind of mother. I was more of a do what I say kind of mother.

I personally feel I was at my best self, raising my children for this season in my life. I had an anointing for it. See, I always wanted to be a mother, and I really enjoyed my children when they were kids, and I still enjoy and love them. As kids, I could tell them what to do. LOL. “Who’s in charge? I’m in charge! Say it again.” This was a line from a movie. I would also repeat that line to myself. So I thought in my head; I had a motto. It was one of me and four of them. They were not going to drive me crazy. I would drive them crazy, LOL.

The true motto was one my grandmother gave me which was to never look at your children as a burden. Only see them as a blessing.

When you perceive a situation as a blessing, your perspective (of it) is always the best. So you think the best, and you are going to get the best, and I did. They are my best work.

That advice came from a woman whose four out of her five children preceded her in death. When I asked her, “How do you get over that grandma?” She shrugged her shoulders and said, "You just did.” Her first child was 6 months when he died. Her twins died 7 days apart as newborns. The first living son was an adult. This adult was my father.

As I continued to heal at this season in life or just move on, as my grandmother would say, I began to assess my situation and view it.

At this point, I’m a master juggler full of fear, or playing the shell game, “where is it now?” I wondered, what if someone finds out I am a juggler. What if I dropped the ball?

What if they see I'm not who they thought I was? The first rule of healing is to get rid of the “What Ifs”. The second rule is who are THEY (that you are so concerned with what they think).

As I stated earlier, I had a checklist for child-rearing. At about midway through this checklist, I began to have severe panic attacks.

Panic attacks come from fear and trauma, unprocessed or just plain old, not dealt with emotion. It will come out one way or the other if you do not deal with it or it will deal with you. I began to manifest some physical illness as well. This is because I am now in complete fear that I am leaving my children.

What seeds did I have inside of me? There were seeds of fear, anger, abandonment, lack, rejection and betrayal. I was on a struggle bus and in a day-to-day survival mode. Truthfully, I was worried. I was worried whether or not I was doing what was right or were we going to be alright. If I could just get them to a certain point, it would be less stressful. I adopted this Scripture for that season:

Matthew 6:25 says don't worry but yet I still had these seeds that have turned into trees unknowingly inside distorting my view: Trauma that had manifested in my body from childbirth, the list could go on. A woman, a prayer warrior, gave me a scripture:

When you pass through the waters, I will be with you; and through the rivers they shall not overflow you. When you walk through the fire, you shall not be burned, nor shall the flames scorch you.

Isaiah 43:2NKJV

You then have to look at what I have demonstrated to my children without speaking a word. What did my energy show them? Was it strength, courage, overcomer, survivor or just human weakness and frailty? I never wanted them to see (fear) in me ("show no fear"). You may possess some fear. However, courage is pressing through the fear!

BUT GOD:

He showed me Grace. What he has predestined, what he has called, these are the results: My children are healthy, intelligent, creative, educated, successful, loving, funny, kind; and the list can go on. They know God. More importantly, God knows them.

I made sure they were taught scripture, prayer, character and how to treat people right. But teaching and growth never stop. Your freedom and those assigned to you are counting on you for you to be your best.

BUT GOD

Chapter 5

Grace

PEACH COBBLER

Peaches Fresh or Canned

Butter

Sugar

Nutmeg

Cinnamon

Flour thickening or slurry

Juices from your peaches

Peaches are the main ingredient in peach cobbler, as well as the healthiest ingredient. Peaches have many benefits in that it is nutrient-rich, protects the immune system, aids in digestion, can help fight cancer, fights allergies and is great for the skin.

And do not be conformed to this world, but be transformed by the renewing of your mind, that you may prove what is that good and acceptable and perfect will of God.

Romans 12:2 NKJV

My father adored me. But the very thing he liked about me was the no-nonsense take no mess boldness that I had. However, he did not like when my mother exhibited these traits (boldness, take no mess).

My father passed in front of me. I felt he was the only protection that I had other than myself.

I was 26 years old. I am now moving into my full adulthood of parenting, struggling with not knowing who I am. This is because I am the master juggler, a hustler in my head and in the head of others. This is because all the balls were in the air.

I know there are some blocks, but I don't know what they are. I would try anything (with moral limits) if it were going to make me money and let me be with my children.

It was like throwing spaghetti at a wall to see which one would stick. I was always chasing something going nowhere and out of breath from the ks).

But God, the on-time God; yes, He sent another ram in the bush. He sent some light for my path.

At this time, I had never heard of Bishop TD Jakes, neither had anyone I knew. My minister was in another state at someone else's church anniversary and Bishop TD Jakes was the speaker.

My pastor asked him to speak at our revival, and He did. Every time I think about that, I think of the scripture when Jesus said if it's just for that one (grace).

And I was that one—Woman Thou Art Loosed.

There were cassette tapes (for those who can remember what those are….) in the lobby of the church. I bought the cassette tape series.

Bishop T D Jakes was the first and only man of God that I was aware of that addressed abuse physically and mentally. He also addressed what spiritual bondage was and is.

That was the first time (to my knowledge) abuse was addressed and talked about in church, and you could be ministered to.

In regard to its impact on your life He ministered on deliverance and light. His ministering on these topics loosed me from the weight of shame, guilt, domestic violence, divorce or the abuse that can happen at any age that the world kept trying to place on me.

At that moment, I realized I had aligned with the view of the world and not with God. As the church folks say, I had a made-up mind. But finally, I, this woman, was loosed.

Our wrongs do not make another person's wrongs ok; it's still wrong.

I was hard on myself with no self-forgiveness or self-love. How could I have picked that person? How could I let that person do that to me? How could I make those decisions? I was looking for someone to save me from where I was in life. When you are in a relationship, dating, friendship or marriage, etc., and that person is broken, and you have some brokenness also, that is a lethal combination.

Let's say you don't have any "brokenness", why do you think you can fix theirs? You go in with a mindset, "I will show them," show them what! How to love and what a good person I am or that you are? You and I are not the sacrificial lamb. Remember Jesus already did that. He sacrificed his life for us all. So when someone tells you or shows you who they are, please believe them!

If I would have stopped and taken responsibility for myself and my life, I would have avoided time wasted. There is an old saying, “All this going around robin's barn to get where you are going wastes time and energy.” I/we have a responsibility to seek God and his promises.

But seek first the kingdom of God and his righteousness, and all these things shall be added to you.

Matthew 6:33 NKJV

But first things first, If I am not seeking Him, the one with the master plan, Jeremiah 29, and I think my plan is better, that is a disaster. I want you to think about how my plan can be greater than the one with the master plan, the master-builder with the blueprint (if you don't knock it off), and go and sit down somewhere and be humble!

Sometimes you have to talk to yourself like that. I was always able to be something or someone in everyone else's life but not my own. How did I not pursue walking in my own truth? Many Christians are in bondage and have not walked in their true identity.

Quote:

No one is coming to rescue you from yourself; your inner demons, your lack of confidence, your dissatisfaction with yourself and your life. Only self-love and good decisions will rescue you.

I would like to add to this quote*: God will send helpers just as He sent the Holy Spirit to guide you. He will not leave you, orphans. And to guide you, there are destiny helpers. This is assistance or an equipping if you will. So the crooked places are made straight. You are still the one who has to* *show up and show out, put the work in, be a vessel. You get where I am going, right?*

BUT GOD

Chapter 6

Recognition

Southwest Chicken Salad

Red grapes

Celery

Poached chicken breast and thighs

Green onions

Walnuts

Mayonnaise dressing

The Holy Spirit moved me one morning to ask God to create in me Lord a clean heart; search me, oh Lord. When those seeds turn into trees and have fruit, we are supposed to bear fruit. The fruit is evidence of your life. That is how I knew about my own life, whether the fruit is bad or do I even have fruit, how much, etc. It's a fruit inspection process.

This fruit inspection process resonates in the song Billie Holiday sings called strange fruit. The song alluded to African Americans being hung from a tree. Picture your soul and all the breaks in it and its offspring. The offenses of the heart are what the enemy tries to trample on. -----The growth in the break(strange fruit you can't recognize it, but it looks familiar) ***The Fruits of the Spirit are Love, joy, peace, righteousness, forbearance, kindness, goodness, gentleness, faithfulness and self-control against such things there is no law.*** **Galatians 5:22-23**

1. Love = for others, my children & family I don't think I had time to have it for myself

2. Joy= What's that? Happiness but happiness is an outward expression. Based on an outside experience.

3.Peace = never / quite time questionable

4. Patience = none. I wanted things to happen NOW

5. Kindness = always tried to show it. Not sure if it came across

6. Goodness = I believed in it

7.Faitfullness= Not to myself / but for others true blue

8.Self-Control= Most of the time

God help me.

9. Longsuffering=yes, I was always helping someone through something and was there for them (and was proud of it).

The seed is within / not on the outside.

My fruits of the spirit lacked because there were other fruits at work. These fruits were a result of the lack of the fruits of the spirit. The actual fruit I was bearing at the time were: fruits of survival, fatigue, unbelief, resentment, lack, lack of trust, pride, depending on myself, codependency, frustration and being quick on the defense with a coke and a smile!

You know I can be so bold for someone else or others but for myself; I would not ask the Lord for me. Was it a lack of expectation or a spirit of disappointment?

When I look at what my belief system was for life, it leaves me speechless. I had to write this down.

I knew what I wanted to say, but this was the truth. You almost say to yourself, all that was in me? Nevertheless, I still work on it (my fruit inspection process) daily. I love God even more because he never gave up on me. He waited for me.

We are not waiting on God he is waiting on us to come to ourselves and senses. This has already been done. This life is waiting on you to access the manifestations. It is waiting for you to believe his word to trust and believe. One of my favorite parts of scripture is when Jesus ***says assuredly, I say unto you.*** *W*hen Jesus says ***assuredly,*** that is a sure thing.

BUT GOD

Chapter7

Completion

Creole Stuffed Puff Pastry-

Creole Blackened Shrimp

Rice

Andouille Sausage

Red Sauce (tomato sauce based)

Smoked Gouda or a pepper jack cheese stuffed into The puffed pastry

Creole seasoning

Matthew 15:13

Jesus replied: "Every plant that my heavenly Father didn't plant is destined to be uprooted.

Creativity was and is a lifeline for me. The framework of my brain processing is creative. I am a creative visionary. I can hear an idea or look at a pattern of colors and bring a room, event or food pairings to life.

God's grip would not let me go. He had his hand on me through it all. Isaiah 43:1-4, message version:

But now, God's message, the God who made you in the first place, Jacob/Stephanie. The one who got you started Israel: Don't be afraid, I have redeemed you. I have called you by name. You're mine.

When you're in over your head, I'll be there with you, Stephanie. When you're in rough waters, Stephanie, you will not go down. When you are between a rock and a hard place, it won't be a dead end. Because I am God, your personal God, the holy of Israel, your Savior. I paid a huge price for you: Stephanie: all of Egypt. With rich Cush and Seba thrown in! That's how much you mean to me! That's how much I love you! I'll sell the whole world to get you back and trade the creation just for you, Stephanie.

I knew this. However, the manifestation of the fruit I was producing in life at times did not reflect the honest truth. The layers of strongholds (in your life) can be nasty sometimes (usually, most of the time). My wrong thought process or perceptions were that I believed I had to do it a certain way, and until I broke the stronghold, I was stuck in the framework of that type of a self-sabotaging mindset.

FRUIT: A farmer checks his fruit. Otherwise, the weeds will seep in, grow up and overtake the good crop.

When you have to be searched, you are forced to walk on a journey of self-awareness. I realized that my false self-perception was based on a lie the devil told me, and I believed it. You start building your life on those lies. This begins in childhood. You think because you are a Christian, you are ok. I didn't know anything about deliverance at this time.

The devil is a liar! Some things I lost because I was afraid to expose what I went through or what I thought. We don't tell our story because it is embarrassing. And we do not want to re-visit the past. This is because it hurts. It just reminds us of a bad time. But it is still a stronghold if not confronted. We only like to tell the parts of our story that are not offensive.

In a class that I recently took with Dr. Tiffany K. Jordan, she discussed that t*here are only two choices of thought: God or the devil.* Dr. Tiffany stated "*So don't flatter yourself to think your thoughts are authentic or original.*" And to paraphrase her statement, *in my mind your thoughts are either, Light or Dark.* .That struck me to really think about my thought patterns!"

Someone asked me why I wanted to cook and where did my love for cooking come from? I always loved to cook. I found it to be an expression of love. It was comforting, and it illuminated the creative giant in me.

When I got married, cooking saved my life. I was in an abusive situation, and cooking was my sanity. Cooking was my sanity to get through all of my life. I would take the newspaper and cut out recipes. I would get recipes from everywhere. I was always attracted to cooking because it fulfilled something in me.

BUT GOD:

It would allow me to focus on creativity and taste. As a business owner, professional chef and event designer, I am walking in my calling. This is another point of success!

(But God)

He has plans (Jeremiah 29)

And His plans override the above. I call it the But God Factor.

I always loved this when I heard it. Because the But negates what's prior to: (BUT GOD).

See, the enemy does not have that kind of power. God is the power. The enemy can only take these kinds of holds by you agreeing and being in alignment with him. One way the alignment gets influenced is through your words. What is on your heart is what comes out of your mouth. The power of life and death is in your tongue. What you think you are, you will speak. This is another source of your power or lack thereof. Your world results in a manifestation of your thoughts.

Death and life are in the power of the tongue, and those who love it will eat its fruit.

Proverbs 18:21. NKJV

BUT GOD

Chapter 8

Abundance

Bloody Mary Ox Tail

Ox Tails

Bloody Mary Mix

Bell Peppers

Green Onion

Garlic

Teriyaki

Carrots

Chili peppers

New Birth of Spirituality

As it is said, “when the student is ready, the teacher will appear”. And yes, I was ready and seeking. Some of the same teachers that I had studied /followed earlier in life, I had an alignment with and their influence definitely seemed to ring true to my spirit. However, at the time I began to follow these teachers, I had some old mindsets that did not seem to work for me (strongholds). I had definitely seen the word of God work, and through my prayers for others that God answered. Things would work for a while for me. And I would find myself in a position of starting over or having to abandon it altogether. Then someone would always say “I don’t understand.” You have what it takes. How is it you are not further along?

I would want to shrink but something would pull me back out. God has to show you the weak areas in you that need to be strengthened in order to take you to the designated areas of life. However, when I became a ready and willing student of the word, that's when the revelation of the truth of the word began to work.

As the layers began to pull off, I could see and hear. Now I could receive an understanding, as some would say, an awakening: *Some Wisdom.*

Titus 1:2

She Judged Him Faithful Who Had Promised.

In hope of eternal life, Which God; That Cannot Lie; promised before the world began.' Although all things are possible with God, but Three Things Are Impossible with Him: He cannot **Lie**, He cannot **Die** and He cannot **Fail.**

I am moving away from a religious state of being and into a relationship state of being.

John 10:10 NKJV

Jesus Speaks: ***The thief does not come except to steal, to kill, and to destroy. I have come that they may have life and that they may have it more abundantly.***

Second half of the scripture in The Passion Translation:

***But I have come to give you everything in abundance, more than you expect - life in its fullness until you overflow*!**

Abundance - A-bun-dance Abundance doesn't just mean money; it is a part of an abundant life.

Abundance- a very large quantity of something plenty; fullness of the good things of life; prosperity.

A-bun- bun two pieces of; -dance- to lead someone in a particular direction while moving (to move rhythmically) : a series of movements that match the speed and rhythm of a piece of.......

The Greek word; for abundant can also mean excess, more than or super flows.

Would I have come to understand is that there are two of us in this dance and I am not the lead?

When you become aware, awareness of your life and who you are! Also, when you become aware of whose you are you decide to be responsible for it (the awareness of your identity and belonging).

We are not meant to just exist in life or survive life. You are to be plentiful in the good things of life.

Abundance of: Love/ Health/ Ideas/ Creativity/ Wealth/Knowledge and Understanding.

BUT GOD

Chapter 9

Breakthrough

Deep-Fried Lobster tail with Creole pasta

Penne Pasta

Bechamel sauce

Onions (diced fine)

Creole Seasoning

Deep-Fried Lobster Tail Tossed in Butter, Lemon and Creole Seasoning

If you are only looking at what you possess, it will never be enough. Your perception is the key to your expectation. But Jesus said, bring them to me. I brought myself to him, my thoughts, my burdens, my worries, my gifts, my imperfections my desires, my hopes. I brought it all. And by bringing it to him, he took it, and looked up to heaven, blessed and broke it. In healing, there is a blessing and a breaking at the same time. It is simultaneously. I believe it to be because I cannot see God leaving your soul dismembered or disfigured.

He is a God of Wholeness. Remember Jesus came to heal the broken-hearted. He will align you with what and who you need. There is a breaking of the old. There is also a receiving or a reception of the blessing.

Every fragment of my life/our lives have meaning. Nothing will go unused. God will take every single piece and put it together and make the perfect meal. Like the cornbread dressing and just like the dressing, all the fragments were molded into a beautiful cuisine. Do you find it strange or a coincidence that it is a meal traditionally served at Thanksgiving? That's Just Food For Thought.

There is a currency of overflow when you give what you have to God. They started out with a small amount, but when they gave it to the miracle worker, he multiplied it until it became an overflow. That is what he wants to do with our faith, truth, belief system and our life. He wants us to surrender them to him.

Although in our finite perception, we may not believe what we have is much. We may be perplexed and wonder how we will be able to make it with what we have. When we think we have come to the end of our road, that's when the breakthrough comes.

We must hold on. He gives us strength. Remember, we are one with God, our father, and we are not separate from the father. We have to surrender to feel the impact of our breakthrough, giving up our old habits and tendencies of wanting to be in control.

We all have had conflict with surrendering at some point or another. There is an inner conflict to surrender because we feel we are giving up our dreams. We think what we barely have is already being taken away. Surrendering to God does not mean giving up the dream. Surrendering the dream to God means you are giving it back to the one who gave you the dream so he can perfect it beyond your imagination!

But the helper, the Holy Spirit, whom the father will bring in My name, He will teach you all things, and bring things to your remembrance all things that I said to you.

John 14:26 NKJV

For Jesus to say that he will bring this to your remembrance, it means you already know. That means this is already a part of you. You have already had a conversation about these things with your spirit. So remember it is spirit to spirit.

For the Holy Spirit makes God's fatherhood real to us as he whispers into our innermost being,

"You are God's beloved child!"

Romans 8:16. The Passion Translation

BUT GOD

Chapter 10

Spiritual Awakening

Cornbread Dressing

Cornbread

Toasted Loaf of Bread

Bell Peppers-Red and Green

Green Onions

Celery'

Sage

Poultry Seasoning

Salt and Pepper to taste

Chicken Stock or Turkey Broth

I heard the spirit of God say to me. This is when you make peace with yourself. And He said I am taking you home, (not to heaven but) home as in the foundation of who you truly are.

Home in this context references the authentic you; the true version of yourself, your son-ship, the one who is created in his image. Just like Jacob, I want to transform you into my image and form you.

This is the goal all along, and it is ongoing. God wants to transform you into His image so that you will feel at home. And remember, there is no other comparison to you. You are unique. Your voice has its own pattern. When you call Him, he says that's my child. He is not confused as to which one you are.

On the contrary your natural parents, they will confuse the names of their children, mix the names, combine the names and then say, you know who I am talking to. But not God, You and God have your own two-step.

You feel a sense of belonging that you are where you are destined to be. It is comforting and restful when you are at home. Until we examine ourselves, confess our (flaws, faults, sins, weakness) and repent - turn from and realign, we will always be stagnant in our destiny.

It is then when He can use us to our full potential.

Just like Jacob wrestled with the angel until He received the blessing, I too had to wrestle (do the work of letting go). Just like Jacob, I had to confess my faults and my sins, flaws, etc. Be honest with yourself because you are not fooling God or your authentic self.

I decided that I was not going to leave until he blessed me.

After the angel wrestled with Jacob, His hip became out of joint/place. Ironically, I had pain in my hip after I confessed.

It was a Jacob confirmation at that moment because God revealed that at the point of confession, I could move forward to destiny and blessing, maximizing my potential.

But just like the disciple, placing it in his hands, and it multiplied, that is the same way we are to put our life, money, future, children's destiny in His hands.

He cannot just be Lord in name only. He has to be the Lord of our Lives, our thoughts, our bank accounts, our children, a movement, or touch.

I want you to be Lord of my thoughts and my intentions, and Lord over my hands. I want my touch to reflect you. When I speak, I want it to reflect you. He has to be Lord of everything.........

Surrendering is a daily process. When he is Lord, you will feed the 5,000 and have 12 baskets left over. Metaphorically, what is your 5,000, and what are your 12 baskets? With the same two fish and five loaves in his hands it is unlimited. So take the limitations off!

I never thought I would say this, but I surrender. I've been in the wrong fight, the wrong boxing ring for what seems like a lifetime and it wasn't my battle.

And they said to Him, "We have here only five loaves and two fish." He said, "Bring them here to me". Then he commanded the multitudes to sit down on the grass. And He took five loaves and two fish, and looking up to heaven, He blessed and broke and gave the loaves to the disciples; and the disciples gave to the multitudes. So they all ate and were filled, and they took up twelve baskets full of the fragments that remain. Now those who had eaten were about five thousand men, besides women and children.

Matthew 14:17-21 NKJV

BUT GOD

Conclusion

I always knew I desired freedom. I just did not know how to access it. I always knew there was an internal source that I possessed. This inner source has graced me with grit, determination and the ability to thrive beyond natural resilience. I would always say to myself I wanted to be free. I wanted freedom. But it almost seemed redundant because I am already free. Let the redeemed of the Lord say so!

My frustration came in because I knew I was hitting a wall. So I would try every external direction. However, the breaking point or open door was not outside of me. But those external directions I kept reaching for to find freedom were just manifestations of thoughts and a belief system.

What I was really searching for to attain freedom was, "ON THE INSIDE!"

It was a WIZ moment, if you will. You might ask "how would I access the truth?" You begin to unpack and lay aside every weight and do not put that suitcase back in the drawer or the closet until it is empty.

Suitcase

A **suit** is a set of outer clothes made of the same fabric and designed to be worn together—the word **case**: one's circumstance or position, an instance or a disease or problem; example of something occurring. Know this the outward man is carrying the situation or dis-ease of the inward man. Unpack! Because once you unpack you can attain "FREEDOM." My freedom is here! It's an awareness! Actually, it's a **Revelation**. Be free of the Lie the Devil Told you and You Believed: BUT GOD!

The eyes of your understanding be enlightened; that you may know what is the hope of his calling, what are the riches of the glory of His inheritance in the saints, and

what is the exceeding greatness of His power toward us who believe, according to the working of his mighty power.

Ephesians 1:18-19 KJV

I pray that the light of God will illuminate the eyes of your imagination, flooding you with light, until you experience the full revelation of the hope of his calling that is the wealth of God's glorious inheritance that he finds in us, his holy ones! I pray that you will continually experience the immeasurable greatness of God's power made available to you through faith. Then your lives will be an advertisement of this immense power as it works through you! This is the mighty power

Ephesians 1:18-19The PASSION Translation

Identity Introduction to Myself:

Hello, my name is Stephanie

Hello Stephanie. My name is Stephanie Dionne (The definition of Stephanie Dionne is: Crown Devine) And it's a pleasure to meet you. I love you and I thank you for your help on this journey. But I must take it from here on. From Stephanie with love,

To console those who mourn in Zion, to give them beauty for ashes, the oil of joy for morning. The garment of praise for the spirit of heaviness: that they may be called trees of righteousness, the planting of the Lord that he may be glorified. And they shall rebuild the old ruins. They shall raise up the former desolations, and they shall repair the ruined cities in the desolations of many generations.

Isaiah 61:3-4 NJKV

Notes

www.ingramcontent.com/pod-product-compliance
Lightning Source LLC
LaVergne TN
LVHW020649100826
845148LV00012B/2400

* 9 7 8 1 7 3 7 8 9 8 3 0 6 *